Nick Wa...
The Surprise Present

Oxford University Press

Oxford Toronto Melbourne

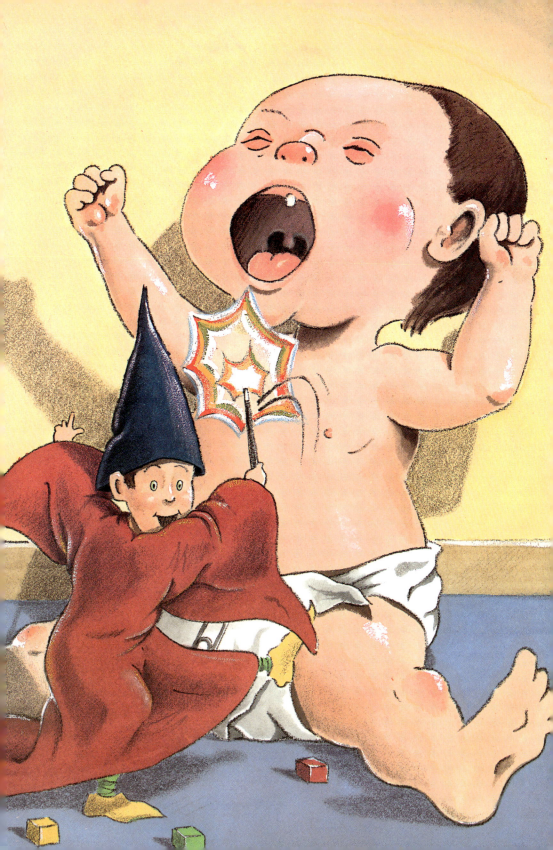

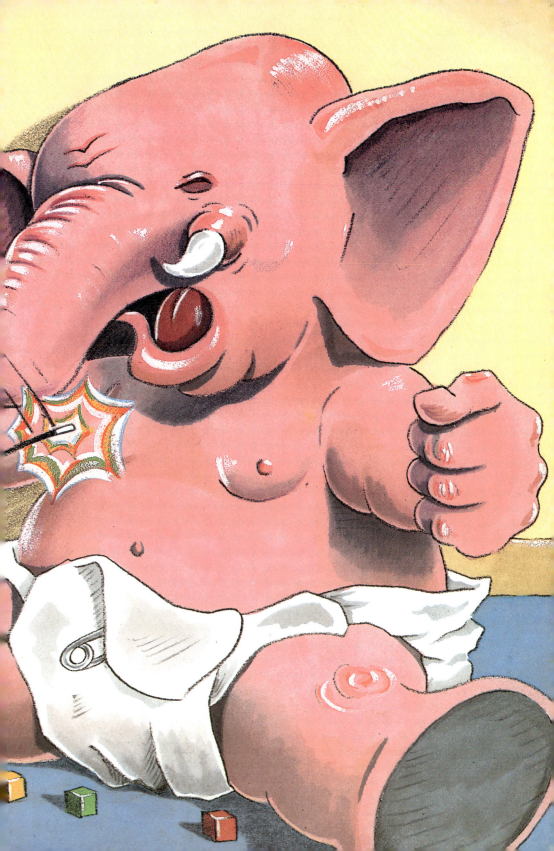

Oxford University Press, Walton Street, Oxford OX2 6DP
Oxford New York Toronto
Delhi Bombay Calcutta Madras Karachi
Petaling Jaya Singapore Hong Kong Tokyo
Nairobi Dar es Salaam Cape Town
Melbourne Auckland

and associated companies in
Beirut Berlin Ibadan Nicosia

Oxford is a trade mark of Oxford University Press

© Nick Ward 1984
First published 1984
Reprinted 1986

British Library Cataloguing in Publication Data
Ward, Nick
The surprise present.
I. Title
823'.914[J] PZ7
ISBN 0-19-272142-9

Printed in Hong Kong